Age - it's just a number

An anthology

from Littleborough U3A

Creative Writing Group

and others

GW00707563

PreeTa Press Ltd

Published by Preeta Press Ltd in 2020
www.preetapress.com

Printed by ImprintDigital.com

FOREWORD

Littleborough U3A Creative Writing Group is just one of the many interest groups that have been formed since the U3A (the University of the Third Age) came to Littleborough in 2014. The third age is that age in a person's life that follows after retirement and semi-retirement. We are a small group who get together twice a month in a relaxed, friendly and informal environment to explore the many aspects of creative writing. We all bring our many and varied experiences in order to learn from each other.

DEDICATIONS AND ACKNOWLEDGEMENTS

We are grateful to Link4Life and Littleborough U3A for funding the project.

To James Nash for curating the anthology

Thank you to all the people who submitted poems, far too many for one small volume.

To Mike Webb for the cover design.

To Rita and Paul from Preeta Press Ltd for their guidance.

INTRODUCTION

Poetry can find the words for the most important of our human experiences. It can shine a light on our own lives and the lives of others. This wonderful collection compiled by Littleborough U3A Creative Writing Group examines the whole inevitable ageing process with honesty, humour and courage. Inevitably memories are tangled up in the writing when poets deal with what it means to grow older.

So, we have poems here that examine what we now see in the mirror, and how it compares to past reflections. We have poems that deal with childhood, poems that deal with loss and bereavement and those that celebrate the essential spirit and beauty that endures even amongst the unavoidable changes that come to our senior selves.

Poets have always dealt with themes of mortality and the natural world, and in describing the changes that the seasons bring the poets here have written wonderful meditations on age and what may come with it.

Some of these poems come from members of the Littleborough U3A group but others come more widely from the borough of Rochdale and represent a range of writing and life experience. You will only have to read a few before you see their beauty and sincerity, and how such an important theme is dealt with so beautifully and in so many different ways.

There are distinct pleasures in both writing and in reading poetry. I am sure that whether a writer or a reader [or both] you will be inspired by the pieces to be found in this anthology.

In conclusion let me borrow the words of Maureen Harrison from her poem, 'The Broken Trumpet', 'Forget the rust, see the beauty'.

James Nash is a writer, journalist and poet. A long-term resident of Leeds and Bridlington, his third collection of poems, Coma Songs was published in 2003 and reprinted in 2006. He has two poems in Branch-Lines [Enitharmon Press 2007] among fifty contemporary poets, including Seamus Heaney and U. A. Fanthorpe.'Some Things Matter', and 'Cinema Stories' were published by Valley Press in 2012 and 2015.

His most recent collection 'A Bench for Billie Holiday: Seventy Sonnets' was published in October 2018.

CONTENTS

MIRRORED REFLECTIONS
Sue Temperley

Our eyes first met when she was quite young.
We pulled strange faces and stuck out our tongue.
We stared and laughed making each other smile
And messed about as we watched all the while.

When she hit fifteen, we still liked to gaze
At our bright green hair which was then all the rage,
And with dark-kohled eyes and dark crimson lips
We would pout and pose - ignoring folks' quip

At twenty-one we checked in all the time
Ensuring the make-up was all good and fine!
Boys came and went and we'd share the odd tear,
But mostly we'd smile 'cos we'd nothing to fear.

Then came the day when we gasped at the sight
Of our faces flushed pink in rapturous delight.
Our eyes bright and sparkling, a white veil hanging down,
We sighed and admired our white wedding gown.

We continued to share our smiles and our joy
And soon we were joined by a fine baby boy,
He gurgled and laughed as he saw both our faces
We watched as he grew and took his first paces.

The years rolled on by and still we would stare
At each other's faces and gasp when a hair
Of silvery grey curled into our view,
Or a tell-tale wrinkle showed what we both knew.

That day when we saw we were wearing all black
The tears wouldn't stop and we just looked back
At our faces so grim with grief and despair,
We had buried her man and life no longer seemed fair.
Our lines became deeper, our hair turned to white,

We looked into our eyes and felt old age bite.
Her hand was unsteady as we smiled that last time
And our reflection slowly faded – it was the end of the line.

THE LEAF
Julie Mills

Life is like a leaf
It unfurls, a new life, vibrant green and fragile
Gaining strength as it grows
Veins run through like a stream
Gently flowing
Billowing softly in the wind
It provides shelter, a sanctuary
For mothers and their young
Mother Nature
A small fleck, in an ever-growing tapestry
Each one unique
The leaf grows
Majestically blooming
Forever changing
On its journey through the seasons
As we are through the years
Spring moves into summer
Autumn draws near
The leaf changes colour
As it grows older with time
Until the wind blows
It falls to the ground slowly
Fluttering like a butterfly
Until finally it settles still
Brittle and crumbling
It's life drawing to a close
Back into the earth

THE BOOK OF LIFE
Rod Broome

In chapter one, a baby's born, and fills a home with joy,
With ribbons for a little girl, or bootees for a boy
A miracle has just occurred, and neighbours flock to see
The new inhabitant of earth, who'll follow you and me.

The child grows up and learns the ropes, and freedom is
the rule,
To run and jump and play at games, and spend some time
at school
But soon the world of work cuts in, and skills need to be
learned
So, its noses to the grindstone, there's money to be earned!

And then one day, a love affair! – a soulmate comes along –
a person for each one of us to whom we can belong,
We make a home together and gladness fills our heart
We find that life in partnership is better than apart.

Co-operation is the task and learning how to share
We have to practice 'give and take' and also 'love and care'
And very soon our twosome turns into three or four
For now, we are a family – put 'FAMILY' on the door.

Too soon the young ones leave us to make their way in life
And we are left just as we were – a husband and a wife
But now we are much older and often need a hand
To vac the house or clean the car or something else we've
planned.

We notice when we drive the car that speeding is the game,
And stairs are getting steeper – it really is a shame!
Our road is getting longer, our bags are heavier too
And people speak so slowly when they talk to me and you.

And so, we're back to childhood, and people gather round

They mime the words close to our face with very little
sound.
We find we've come full circle, we have our fireside chair
The world goes on around us, and leaves us settled there.

THE BROKEN TRUMPET
Maureen Harrison

How dirty, bent and forlorn are you
lying there for all to see?
What tales you could tell are hidden from view.
What life did you lead before your fall?

When you were new did you gleam
and sparkle with pride?
Were your notes pure and true,
did you fill the air with ecstasy?

What happened that you are so bent?
Did someone on you their temper vent?
Is that what makes you what you are -
a broken, twisted instrument?

You may be shabby, tired and woeful.
Yet look more closely and see the life
once flowing through the thing you were.
Forget the rust, see the beauty.

THE FACE
Gail Campbell

I glance into the mirror,
I stop – what do I see?
The face reflecting back,
Can surely not be me?
Fine lines frame thinning lips,
Skin no longer tight.
The blue eyes – well they look like mine,
But don't seem quite as bright.
I move a little closer,
And touch my greying hair,
And then I smile as now I see
The person who is there.
The lines reflect the laughter
I've had throughout the years,
And yes, there are some little lines
That came from shedding tears.
My eyes have seen such wonders,
The memories so clear.
Good times, bad times, part of life,
But all of it held dear.
I look again, and laugh out loud,
As suddenly I see,
My mother's face, so soft and round,
Is smiling back at me.
And I'm content with this old face,
It's what it's meant to be.
This face is proud, this face is fine,
This face belongs to me.

A LIFE OF DEDICATION
Fran Moir

I have been with you for a very long time
Since you were handsome & in your prime
I knew even then that you were insecure
But I could help you with that I was sure

I had to be strong for you, you know
There were many times when you were low
I would do my best bring you back
I think I have that special knack

Do doubts creep into your mind
Is that why you are often unkind?
You are always pulling me this way and that
It's as if you are waiting for me to snap

You know I haven't ever complained
Even with all of the extra strain
I know because of our familiarity
You would find it hard to replace me

Those days you felt safe with me
This is something we didn't foresee
But I am feeling so frail & weak
That our future is looking bleak

I realise the relentless truth
We can't go back to the times of our youth
I have never let you down before
I have always kept you safe & secure

You forget that I am getting old
You're ageing too if truth be told
I am at the point of breaking
It's time for some decision making

Let's face it my long-time friend
This relationship is coming to an end
I think you need the embraces
Of a new pair of braces!

MIRROR, MIRROR
Janet Taylor

Who is that woman I see each day?
It definitely can`t be me
She has wrinkles and grey hair
And I do not

This woman has a care worn face
With eyelids drooping heavily
Her lips pursed in disapproval
And I do not

This woman has eyes that shine
There`s mischief in that twinkle
I think I know her face
I do.

AGEING THOUGHT FOR THE DAY
Sue Temperley

Think on this:
With age comes wisdom -
Comfy shoes, elastic waists,
Selective deafness.

TWILIGHT
Catherine Coward

Memories are foggy,
faces more and more vague,
mirrored image just stares,
and stares, and stares.

Time is of no essence,
days they matter not,
I repeat what I have said,
a lot,   a lot,   a lot.

Struggling, trying to remember who I am,
who I was and where I began.
twilight beckons, darker every day.
Have I eaten?
Does it matter anyway?

People look at me with pity,
get angry when I stray,
shout when my shoes
are on the wrong way.
Does it matter anyway?

I am wet, it must have rained,
voices shouting yet again.
I **don't** want to bathe,
but they bathe me anyway.
I do **not** want to go to bed,
but in my bed, I'm forced to stay.
Twilight beckons more each day,
grey matter withering like trees in fall,
every day the forest darkens
as I lose my way once more.
Over roots I trip and stumble,
the more I fall, the more I grumble.

Lost in a field of strangers,
Just trying to get home,
voices will not leave me alone,
but I feel so **alone, alone, alone.**

NEW LIFE
Ellen Cruise

Left In the corner old and forgotten
Laces lost and canvas torn
They once were a girl's pride and joy
But now so battered and worn.

Their purpose now served
No tripping the fantastic light,
The pattern of flowers sullied and dull
All a bit of an ugly sight.

But suddenly a hot breath near
Picked up by a mouth so soft
Carried away and thrown in the air
He jumps to catch it aloft.

For the tatty old shoes, a new life begins
As Rover this treasure has found.
Out in garden he chews and gnaws
They are loved by this happy old hound.

THE ALLERTON OAK (CALDERSTONES PARK, LIVERPOOL)

Susan Turner

This tree has stood here for a thousand years
Its trunk is split, it needs support,
Fencing protects it, and so it thrives.
Tourists take selfies, then depart
But an old man lingers on a bench.
Recalls the letters his mother sent
With leaves and acorns from this tree
To his father fighting overseas
Whom he'd never met and never would.
Their message: we will remember you.

But - how do you remember
What you've never known?

In a child, first a void, then anger grows
Twisted and gnarled
As an old tree's limbs.
He went down paths he now knows were wrong
And what might have been he'll never know.
Yet, he knows his children turned out right,
Great grand-kids now light up his life,
So, he can forgive that card he was dealt.
This tree has stood here for a thousand years.

TIME
Rod Broome

When I look back, what do I see?
A lovely girl who's chosen me.
A photograph: she's at my side.
A wedding dress: she is my bride.

Now time has flown, two children play,
A new step forward every day.
Domestic duties dominate
And leave no time to meditate

Soon middle age arrives, and then
We try to plan our lives again,
But now our parents need us more,
They're old and frailer than before.

Our children grow and very soon
Form little families of their own,
And tiny tots are here again
Who play at 'house' or 'on the train.'

Old age arrives, and sad to say
Our friends or loved ones pass away,
But we are glad we've had the chance
To play a part in life's rich dance.

And when my time comes to depart
A thankfulness will fill my heart
For all the blessings in my life:
A home, a faith, a loving wife.

THE CLOCK TICKS
Janet Taylor

She is born
And takes her first breath
The clock begins to tick
Ageing has begun

She grows strong
She walks and talks
School beckons
The clock ticks

She`s working now
She`s met a boy
Marriage maybe
The clock ticks

She`s a mother
A family of her own
She loves her life
The clock ticks

Her children grow strong
She loves and guides them
She`s a proud mum
The clock ticks

She`s alone now
They have all grown and gone
Her time has come
The clock stops

PRIVATE 241602

Gail Campbell

I'm happy now I know you're here.
Come closer, please, no need for fear.
I've waited such a long, long time,
To meet you future girl of mine.
You talk to me through all your tears.
Has it really been a hundred years,
I've rested here to await the day,
My future girl would come my way?
They said the end was just in sight.
To defend our country was only right.
In foreign land be brave and bold,
And fight in rain, in sleet, in cold.
I thought of home, where I should be.
My wife, my kids, my family.
And I was sad, because I knew,
My life on earth would soon be through.
I wouldn't see my hair turn grey,
Or walk out on a sunny day,
Or hold a grandchild close and tight,
Or live to see another night.
So future girl, you live your life.
There will be struggles, there will be strife.
But ageing has no guarantee,
I thought it did, but look at me.
I'm Private 241602,
And I'll be looking out for you.
I live in you, you have my eyes.
No one ever really dies.
Though I'll not age like most men do,
I'll still be here because of you.
My future girl, you feel it too,
The love that passes from me to you.

SALLY
Elizabeth White

She watched him
As he entered the room
He stood straight and tall
Army she thought
He walked towards her
This seat taken he asked
No she replied

John he said
Holding out his hand
Sally she said, ignoring it
Around the room
Eight pair of eyes watched
Drawn by the unusual activity
Countdown forgotten

Unable to resist
She turned to look at him
Warm brown eyes gazed at her
The room swam
Forgotten feelings surged
She was 16 again
At her first dance

You're new she said
Respite, she queried
permanent he said
Kids thought it best
He rested his arm on her chair
The touch of his body
Warming her

Sally ready for your bath
Shouted the carer

The mood was broken
She blushed
Scrub your back said a voice
Cheeky she replied
Her dignity restored

GETTING ON A BIT
Steve Lister

Where did that belly come from?
It wasn't here not long ago!
I've just realised my waist has re-sized
And I can no longer see my big toe.

I used to be quite fit and healthy
I'd run seven miles every day
But now in the morning I just lie there yawning
My legs are just wasting away

I used to be good at karate
At tai chi and judo and such
But since my last grading my energy's fading
I just can't be bothered that much.

It feels like the end of the party
When it's time to sup up and go.
But hang on a minute, I haven't quite finished
I'm learning to play the banjo!

MY GREEN LEGACY
Marilyn Aldred

Look at me, nearer to eighty,
than twenty-three.
These wrinkles, like the rings of a tree
give you a clue to my longevity.
Unlike a tree, tall and strong
my days are numbered,
can't say how long.

So, every day brings such joy for me
as I survey my legacy.
The trees I've planted across the years.

The sapling Oak,
I planted when twenty-three.
Back then the same height as me.
'tis now hundred feet or more,
half a Century I've watched it soar.
The cornerstone of a green fortress
which surrounds my home.

The Sycamore a gift from Dad,
struggles through winters so bad,
branches snap off under the weight of snow.
When spring comes and it bursts into leaf.
I remember Dad and sigh with relief.
In spring the Cherry Blossom and Lilac bring particular
pleasure.
So many trees, so many memories I treasure.
Life is short and when I've gone,
no echo of me will linger on.

ABOUT FACE
Susan Turner

Unafraid to record
The melancholia of ageing -
A facial feature in itself
As real as ears, mouth, nose -
Rembrandt unflinchingly
In his self-portraits urges
'This is me, at this stage in my life',
His works are revered for their
Bravery and truth as much
As for their technical perfection.

But in real life, not Art,
The world has a problem
With you 'looking your age'.
Youthful facial beauty
Is desirable, bankable, marketable.
Perfection is a face on which
Love, loss or life have taken no toll.
All signs of our journey to mortality
Must be eradicated by air-brush,
Injection or the surgeon's knife.
My aged face, untreated, cannot lie.
I have lived. I might as well be invisible

SENIOR MOMENTS

Ian Aitchison

My memory's started to crack
And a sense of direction I lack
If I'm leaving home
My dog has to come
As he always knows the way back.

It's tough with incontinence too
And some things I can't always do
I always demand
The Gents is to hand
Oh sorry! – I just need the loo!

I'll drop off to sleep just for fun
After putting the frying pan on
I'm roused with a cough
Smoke alarm's just gone off
Good job I like bacon well done.

In old age I'm backing the Greens
Foul gases let's cut by all means
We need to make sure
The atmosphere's pure
So, I'm cutting down on baked beans!

I could win a fun run at last
I've often dropped out in the past
Now us OAPs
Might have dodgy knees
But mobility scooters are fast!

And having a bath is a chore
When I can't lift my foot off the floor
Must go to the gym
And get back in trim
Can't get my leg over no more!

SYLVESTER
Rene Wood

Sylvester climbs through the cat flap,
He's glad to get in.
He dribbles saliva down his chin
And his once fat body is thin
His food is mashed as he struggles to chew
With his teeth, as there are few.
He lies on her lap and stretches his paws
She winces when he digs in his claws
He closes his eyes and starts to purr
When she rubs her hands in his fur.
His coat is grey, soft and warm on her fingers
The smell of his rancid breath lingers.
His whiskers twitch as he falls asleep
And dreams, when his sleep is deep
Of a time when he could chase balls on a string
Climb curtains and swing.
Leap on high shelves and jump down with a spring
But now he is content to be
Curled up tightly on Olga's knee.

AND THE SUN ALWAYS SHONE
Carol Ashworth

Oh, I wish I could be beside the sea, back in 1953
Mum, Dad and me, Morecambe was the place to be
The air was good for Mum's bad chest
The entertainment was the best
And the sun always shone

I don't remember PC in 1953
The open-air swimming pool, what a treat
To watch the beauty competitions and choose our best
And hope the judges were impressed
And the sun always shone

In the morning Dad and me
Would go out early and smell the sea
We'd go to a cafe and drink tea
I'd play my favourite juke box tune
And the sun always shone

Every day we'd see a show or maybe even two
There was always lots to see and do
From our digs close at hand
At the end of the pier or the bandstand
And the sun always shone

How I wish I could be beside the sea back in 1953
When the sun always shone

A DESTINY CALLING
Chloe-Emma Jones

Some try and run, some try and hide,
But unfortunately, it can't be denied.
A reversal of roles, from young to old.
A struggle to hear the words you are told.
Relying on loved ones to help you get by.
Reminiscing with all as we laugh and we cry.
Everything changes as the years do go on.
Where has that young girl inside of me gone?
Appearance now differs and health that has faded,
Gone is my youth that I seem to have traded.
Wrinkles, grey hair and pensions galore,
Things I now know that I didn't before.
Your life is a story and you're the main part.
Your destiny mapped out from the very start.
It happens to us all, I'm sure you'll agree.
It's bound to soon happen to you and to me.
Take it in its glory, it's something to be enjoyed.
Something that none of us can ever avoid.
So, look in the mirror and be proud of who you see.
What's been and gone, was meant to be

THE DISMAL DUTY
Margaret Edwards

'Sorry, pet' she said,
handing me my mother's keys
'It's a dismal duty,
clearing out your old family home'
I smiled, determined to calmly
record any items to be kept,
those for charity shops,
those to be left for house clearance.

Stepping into the kitchen, I find
a time-capsule of the 1950s;
My eyes fall on a stack of well used
mixing bowls, an enamel bread bin,
a tiny fridge wedged
awkwardly against the pantry door.
No delicious smells from freshly baked
scones, cakes and biscuits
        fill this chill, airless room.

The sight of a plate of buttered toast
uneaten on the table bring back
bring back memories of when
this room was my childhood refuge.
I abandon my task and leave
the family home for the last time.

THE WOODEN BENCH
Elizabeth White

In the park
On top of the hill
The wooden bench
stands alone

In memory of Joe
The gold plaque says
The words faded
by the sun

A Teddy-bear
sits on the seat
For my granddad
Says the card

As dawn rises
A lady arrives
Leaves a poppy
On the bench

She blows a kiss
Wipes away a tear
Memories fresh
In her mind

Breathing heavily
from the climb
An old man sits
To remember

As dusk falls
All is quiet and still
A fox curls up
Keeping Joe company

On the Wooden Bench

THE MULTIPLICATION OF SEASONS
Lynn Lovell

I will age like a great house,

A house sitting comfortably on a grassy hillside, rooms
And corridors sheltering clear eyed happy children, wings
Wide for those who need sanctuary; sparkling
Windows signalling hope.

Years will pass
I will watch contented
Counting the multiplication of seasons, seeing
The slender saplings I have planted blossom into
Fine tall trees, accepting new paths that lead away
Year by year

But in the end, the cruelty of time will collapse my roof,
Ivy choking pipes, moss and weeds clogging
Gutters, age spots of lichen blotching my face.

Slowly my edifice will collapse brick after crumbling brick
Tumbling into rubble until I crouch,

A derelict pile waiting to be bulldozed
Into history

Leaving only a half
Remembered landmark with
Scarred land and one fallen
Carved stone to mark my tenancy.

I AM LIKE AUTUMN
Andrea Sarginson

I am like Autumn…
Toil weary, introspective and preparing for the winter of my
life.
But, for a while, my spring and summer labours evidence
their yield
In shows of brilliance against the dark, declining days and
baleful haze
And all I was and hoped to be is caught, suspended
fleetingly in this,
My autumn!

Once…
My days were golden with the sweet fruit expectations of
the orchard.
Fruit that formed in young, spring days, blossom pink with
promise.
Fruit that matured in the long, cobalt high sky's, ardent
days of summer;
Fruit that weathered storms and assailants to swell and
colour-deepen,
In my autumn.

Soon…
When the trees stand resting, cold and cheerless and all is
hoary white,
I shall rekindle moments of memory and feel them,
crackling and sparky,
Bonfire incandescent, illuminating my dimness with
gorgeous reds and yellows,
Fed by the bounteous beauty of my spring, my summer, my
harvest,
In winter.

But today…
In the gathering of my life,
My hurts are salved. I feel renewed and golden glorious in
wise maturity.
I marvel at my fruits and hold their colour richness to my
heart.
I gaze on natures bruised and fallen gifts to seek once more,
my life
and finally, I toss away to gently mould, the humus and
detritus of the past…
Now - in my autumn.

I SWORE THE DAY WOULD NEVER COME THAT I'D TURN INTO MY MOTHER
Janna May

When I was young, I swore I'd never
Let my hair turn grey
Or leave the house without my lippy
I'd not wear vests, or God forbid flat shoes
So – now my hair is pink
My clothes extreme
I'm the ageing village hippy!

THE AGEING YEAR
Wendy Lockwood

The changing seasons
 in our northern hemisphere
 bring cold shorter days,

This is visible
as each sunrise creeps southward
along the skyline.

Autumn's equinox
marks nature's preparations
for winter's long sleep.

Rebirth at new year
gradually offers hope
as Spring approaches.

Youthful life bursts through –
or should - unless already
balance is destroyed.

NO END TO MY TALENTS
Ian Aitchison

I once knocked out limericks for fun
But with old age that last line won't come
It's a terrible shock
When you get writer's block …

THE MING VASE
Fran Moir

The bench is austere
Offering little comfort
She rests there
An elegant lady
Her cane propped against her knee
She gazes at the display
As she has so many times before
It sits on a simple wooden plinth
Milky white & cobalt blue
Ming porcelain
She knows this temple jar
Was crafted five centuries earlier
It is no longer perfect
Its surface is crazed with tiny lines
There are scars
From repairs to keep it whole
It had once had a function
Now it is obsolete
Too fragile to be of any use
Nevertheless, of great value
A precious object
People pass with hardly a glance
Overlooking the timeless beauty
Oblivious to the rich history
Or the generations of service
Her filmy eyes once so vibrantly blue
Betray her composure with tears
That trace the lines
On her ivory face
She rises concealing the effort
Grateful for the support of her cane

She walks away with dignity
A woman of no value?

OLD AGE DEFIED!
Ken Hall

We grow old which is inevitable.
Do we have to live to old age!
I have no intensions to grow old!
I play walking football.
I walk at the seaside and the countryside.
I joined social groups if I wish.
Try my hand at creative writing.
Volunteer my time to help others.
Go on holidays on my own or not.
Some of us may grow old without full health.
Some of us may grow old with full health.
I have no intentions to stop.
Come what may I will not stop.
I may grow old gracefully or not.
I am not ready to give in yet.
Live life to the full.
I refuse to grow old alone.
You will never know when that will stop!
I will not stop.
Old age! What is that?

DARKNESS UPSTAIRS
Maureen Harrison

I retreat to darkness upstairs as voices clamour
around me
to decide my fate.
Do they no longer see
me as a person but rather as a toy to be cast aside?
Are my wishes of no interest to them?

No point listening to this discussion.

Darkness upstairs
is far more pleasant;
reliving my life, once joyous and sweet.

So, go ahead and decide what you will.
I have outlived my usefulness to you,
but when I have departed from this life you will love me,
again, for who I once was.

For now, you will do
as you perceive to be right and I
will shelter in darkness upstairs where you cannot
reach me
to hurt me again.
To memories of my youth
I will return.

BYGONE AGE
Ellen Cruise

It once stood proud that building
With congregation vast
But look how years have taken toll
And now its glory past.

Broken window, doors are barred
Stonework rots away
Overgrown the garden roses
No welcome place to-day.

Look close, and you will see
A date upon a stone
The wonderous day this place was born
But now, aged and alone.

Weather beaten and vandalised
Love does not abide
Within its crumbling walls
No beauty glorified.

An empty tower, no bells inside
No hymns sung aloud
The bulldozer awaits in readiness
And stands a farewell crowd.

THE AGEING PROCESS
Julie Mills

You may think I'm being a bit over dramatic
With all the products I buy
But he who laughs last laughs the longest
As cream after cream I apply
I have day cream and night cream
Anti-ageing stuff too
Illuminating gel
What a hullabaloo
I sit every morning
Doing an exercise regime
Then patiently layer on
Cream after cream
I massage the stuff in
Til I can't feel my skin
Into wrinkles and grooves
And the big double chin
My Husband says 'Darling
You are fine as you are'
As I scoop a big handful
Out of the jar
Now don't get me wrong
It's not everyone's wish
To have a face nice and soft
And a pout like a fish
But growing old gracefully
Is not something I do
So, I'll leave all those wrinkles
And frown lines to you

OLD FRIEND
Margaret Edwards

She rests on her favourite chair,
my trusted friend for over a decade
She tries to move
but falls back down
betrayed by weakened legs.

I stroke her tired head
thankful for so many years
of loyal companionship
There is anxiety
in her wide brown eyes
lying, I whisper that she
will be alright.
Grasping her paw,
I nod to the vet
and quickly turn away to face
my life alone.

WHO ARE YOU?
Steven White

Pull the thread, rewind the tape.
Replay the moment.
Press play; a final goodbye.
My search is over,
I have found her; a hopeful smile.
Her first words, *"Who are you?"*

Round a different corner.
Another thread pulled, the tape rewinds
a door opens; a faded picture.
A new conversation, *"Welcome home Son"*
Her beaming smile
all is well, life goes on.

The tape is lost, no warm embrace.
No more threads to pull.
We are strangers, she recognises no-one.
I'm not bitter, at least I tried.
"Hello mum."

BEREAVEMENT
Robin Parker

Morning can sometimes break a fragile heart,
That kindly sleep relief has been and gone;
Awakening hammers home we are apart,
For you have passed and I have slept alone.
Undying love which took us to great heights,
So passionate we barely stopped for breath;
Who could have thought that cruel illness might
Strike one so healthy down to early death?
Bright streaks of dawn no longer light my love,
But shroud the utmost dark of inner pain;
It makes no sense to pray to one above,
For that could never bring you back again.
Though life-times in this scheme of things are brief;
Bereavement is an existential grief.

THE LOCKET
Glenis Meeks

Inside, faded photos lie side by side.
Of a different age. Of a different era.
Unrecognisable now as the people they were,
yet the photos help memory come clearer.
I remember that day and the dress I was wearing,
pretty blue flower print, ideal in the sun,
and he with his quiff and his so sparkly eyes.
Our budding romance had just begun.

Like our marriage, this locket has endured.
Gifted to me, one Valentine's Day.
A token of love, a golden heart,
expressing true fidelity.
Filigree etched in the locket's face,
still fresh, unblemished by time.
Whilst imprints of elderliness adorn our own.
Impressions of life sublime.

To open the locket, is to glimpse
a window on when we were young.
A time of hope, a wide, open future,
but now the pendulum's swung.
We look to the past, times shared, fun had,
as we face our infirmness and pains.
The locket closing ends nostalgia.
And aged reality remains.

I FORGOT
Sylvia Anne Jones

I forgot lots of things
And kept saying to you
"Oh, I forgot to tell you"
Then, worse
I started to tell you again
When you said
"I know this, you told me
Before tea"
Did I?
I don't remember that
Did you feed the cat?
"I Did "you said
"Well she doesn't seem
To think so"
I said
"Perhaps she forgot
she'd already eaten it"
"There" I said "You see,
 it's not just me"
"What"?
"What I just said", I said
"Tell me again"
"I Forgot"

AGEING CAME TO STAY
Bernie Bye

Well I'll be honest Ageing, when you came to stay,
I didn't realise you'd be such a pain.
Trying your damnedest to stop the life that I love,
you were no better when you stayed with mum.
Had to be carried upstairs in the end,
I'd like to say eating was her only friend.
But she ate like a pigeon, peck here peck there,
treated food like medicine, not cordon bleu.

That's what you did Ageing, to a very proud woman,
born in the workhouse, when life failed her mother.
Window dresser by day, watching incendiaries at night,
a wren in Oxford and mother of five.

Her mother, my grandmother, was one of eight,
as a baker and confectioner, she became first-rate.
But in a cruel twist of fate, to the workhouse she went,
when her mother's life on earth was too soon spent.
But she worked on the railways during the war,
and invested in an HMO.
Renting to family members in need,
who would otherwise have ended up on the streets.

Her mother, my great grandmother, took in washing to
survive,
bringing up eight children alone when her husband died.
Renting premises as a bakery was a master stroke,
until she was laid out on the counter and the lease was
revoked.

All good stock, women who won't give up easily,
don't think for a minute it'll be easy, believe me.
My gnarled fingers make Computing and Bridge
battlegrounds,

but I'm determined to resist, as my ancestors were renowned.
I've given up the Walking Group, but don't be fooled,
I can still trip a Fandango on Wednesday's with Hoolio.
I'm terrible at the Thursday quiz but wipe the smirk off your face,
it's just not my forte - not my age.

If you insist on staying, Ageing, you have been warned.
Don't think that your meddling will cause me alarm.
Can't sit here talking to you all day, it's Friday at the U3A.
Spanish for Beginners with Hoolio, I have to go, nos vemos.

MY GRANDMOTHER'S BUTTON BOX
Steve Lister

My Grandmother's button box sat on the sideboard
That stood in the corner by the big black range.
Beside it was a photograph, a young man in uniform;
They said it was my daddy on the day he went to war,

I played with the button box while sitting in the rocking chair
With dough in the oven of the big black range
Later there was warm bread and running golden butter
While my granny sewed my trousers that I had lately torn

The treasures in the button box were mystical and magical
I counted and I weighed them by the big black range
Granny did her knitting while sitting in the rocking chair
Grandad read the paper and the dog licked my feet

I played in the garden in my granddad's potting shed
While he was gently snoring by the big black range
There were hammers, there were chisels and things for mending work-boots
And a smell of oil and polishes and old plant pots.

I walked with my granddad by the smelly River Calder
While Granny stayed home polishing the big black range
The waters of the Calder were dark and odoriferous
They smelt of oil and chemicals and long dead fish

We went into the smithy where he shaped the glowing iron
He showed me tongs and hammers and horseshoes he had made
He brewed a mug of tea on the fires of his forges
And we shared a bag of toffees as the sun went down

We bought a new computer for our growing grandsons
They each have an iPad and can work the video
I think about the button box, the black range and the potting shed
And wonder if it's better than it was so long ago

CONTRASTS
Catherine Coward

Luxurious warm water washes softly
over gnarled arthritic hands,
sweet scent of soap contrasts
with icy water and carbolic of past times.

Softest water soothing nodulus fingers
each painful knot a reminder of past toil,
everyone in unison with Maslow's
Motivation Theory.

Scented sheets, crisp and fresh,
contrast vividly with DDT
sprinkled, lavishly on flannelette.

Air deodorized in pulses
where Jeyes Fluid once reigned supreme.
Hands chapped and raw,
now smothered in cream.

Reflections flicker as,
Like tears, water turns to drops
visions stop as taps turn off

TELL ME WHAT I AM
Ruth-Anne Shoker

Am I weak?
Is this frail frame
a failing replica
of what it used to be?

Wrinkles worn heavily on my skin,
age spots peering through lines,
skin tags labelling my design
as used goods?
Or good for nothing
but to sink in the clouds
of foggy memories
and overcast vision.

Is each passing year
falling inelegantly on me,
like sand clashing
through the hour glass?
Time stealing who I used to be,
stealing my prime
and my beauty.

Easily bruised skin
as easily as my
fragile core within
that strives to keep me
as a bystander to the youth,
a reflection of what will
be true of them someday.
Is this all that I am?

OH, THE 'JOY' OF AGEING...
Chris Thornton

Eyes fail,
Joints creak,
Hearing loss,
Deformed feet.
Clinic visits,
Ops delayed,
Condescension,
Taxes still paid.
Loss of loved ones,
Grief untold,
Feeling useless,
Often cold.
Memory failing,
Misplaced keys,
Toilet visits,
Dodgy knees.

Oh, the 'joy' of ageing...

BUT, pension taken,
Mortgage paid,
Travel pass,
Death delayed.
Flu jabs free,
Bowel cancer screens,
Fuel allowance,
Despite your means.
Time to linger,
Take in the view,
Chat to neighbours,
You hardly knew.
A grandchild's smile,
Those friends of old,
A full life lived,
Old tales retold.

Oh, the JOY of ageing!